MW01611464

The Winning Church

By
Jean-Paul Engler

MARK BARCLAY
PUBLICATIONS
P.O. Box 588 • Midland, Michigan 48640-0588

Kingdom
Ministry Publications
877-286-6372
www.kingdomgroup.net

All scripture quotations are taken from the New King James Version of the Bible. Copyright © 1982 by Thomas Nelson, Inc. Used by permission. All rights reserved.

The Winning Church
ISBN 0-944802-44-3
Copyright © 2006 Jean-Paul Engler

FSCO—Jean-Paul Engler
PO Box 423
New Market TN 37820
865-475-9454
www.fscoministries.org

Published by Kingdom Ministry Publications
2495 Cedar St., Suite 8-b, Holt, MI 48842
(877) 286-6372 kingdomgroup.net

In association with

Mark Barclay Publications
P.O. Box 588, Midland, MI 48640-0588
www.marktbarclay.com

Printed in USA. All rights reserved under International Copyright Law. Contents and/or cover may not be reproduced in whole or in part in any form without the express written consent of the author.

CONTENTS

FOREWORD BY MARK T. BARCLAY

This newest book by Jean-Paul Engler, The Winning Church, is an absolute "must read" for every believer. I also recommend that every pastor everywhere has the opportunity to ponder its contents.

This book was written with great understanding of the local church and presented in a way that not only the average believer can understand but also the most biblically educated. The book addresses several topics that are so important to our future in America and around the world-topics such as the ministry, teamwork, and being workers together in God.

Jean-Paul Engler, with his many years of experience in the ministry as well as living on the mission field, has done an extraordinary job of putting this book together. I believe The Winning Church will be a great blessing to the body of Christ. I salute the author, and I thank him for his research and for sharing this with the rest of us.

May the Lord touch you as you read through each page and encourage you to walk in love and unity and be a great disciple for Jesus Christ!

Dr. Mark T. Barclay
Midland, Michigan

1

HOW DO WE STAND UP TO INSPECTION?

Behold, the Lord stood on a wall made with a plumb line, with a plumb line in His hand.

Amos 7:7

The introduction of this book speaks of the Church as being the bride of Christ. I am convinced that the Body of Christ is now going through the equivalent of a "dress rehearsal." This preparation is absolutely necessary in anticipation of the actual uniting of the Church with the Bridegroom, our Lord Jesus.

In Matthew 25:1-13, Jesus speaks clearly, graphically, and somewhat frighteningly about the condition of the Church in the last days. We're told about ten virgins on their way to meet the Bridegroom. We discover that all ten were virgins and that all ten were carrying lamps. But in the end, only the wise virgins were allowed to enter the Kingdom of Heaven. I certainly hope the 50 percent rejection mentioned in these verses does not reflect the actual failure rate of the Church when Jesus returns!

In the passage of scripture in Amos 7:7 above, the Lord uses construction terms to speak to His people. It's as though God was doing the inspection of a building.

Throughout the Bible, we find God telling His people how they're faring in light of His expectations. At times, the verdict was so severe that total annihilation seemed to be the only solution. In other instances, as in the Book of Ezra, a collective and spontaneous act of repentance decisively solved the problem. God's people were again on their way to abundant blessing and prosperity.

> *Because you say, 'I am rich, have become wealthy, and have need of nothing'-and do not know that you are wretched, miserable, poor, blind, and naked...*
>
> Revelation 3:17

The most recent occasion of God's evaluation of the Church is found in the Book of Revelation. Some of the local churches mentioned there evidently performed better than others. One, however, stands out like a sore thumb! It is the Church of Laodicea. The fact that the

Lord would threaten to vomit them out of His mouth is certainly bad enough. But what is even more tragic is that this church isn't even aware of its backslidden condition! Indeed, by its own estimation, it thinks of itself as a church that's doing extremely well!

If Jesus were to do the inspection of the spiritual house we call the Church today, what would His verdict be? In terms of impacting society, its purity, its glory, and its ability to inspire awe and respect from the world, what score would He give the Church today?

Depending on whom you ask and what criteria you use to measure the maturity and performance of the Church today, you might come up with very different results.

> *But they, measuring themselves by themselves,*
> *and comparing themselves among themselves,*
> *are not wise.*
>
> 2 Corinthians 10:12

Although the Apostle Paul strongly urges us not to measure our performance by comparing ourselves to others, I'm afraid that's exactly what the Church has been doing for the past 2000 years.

This reminds me of something I saw many years ago, while vacationing with my family at a popular Central

American beach resort. The construction of what was to be a 15-plus-story hotel was going on near the ocean. While only four levels were built, you could already tell there was something terribly wrong with that construction. The first floor seemed to be fairly level. The outside walls of the second leaned quite noticeably to the left. But not to fear, the third level walls leaned so much to the right that it more than compensated for the second floor "mistake!" The outside walls of the fourth floor seemed perfectly straight. For someone checking the walls on the fourth floor, everything would have seemed okay. But to the building inspector standing outside and across the street, everything beyond the first level would have to come down and be rebuilt!

When churches compare themselves to other churches, they often come up with a distorted view of themselves. For example, when attendance noticeably increases in church "A," the pastor of that congregation may feel like he's doing well, compared to churches "B" and "C," who just lost a considerable number of people because of a split or some other internal turmoil. But if only a few people were brought into the Kingdom during that time period, there was, in fact, no growth at all. What actually happened is what is called "lateral growth." This is the process by which church "A" experiences an increase in attendance because churches "B" and "C" have lost a corresponding number of members! A much more accurate indicator would have been to count how many first-time decisions were actually made during the attendance surge.

I can't help but wonder how Jesus sees the Church today. After all, He's its builder. If indeed His "building codes" are different from ours, what will He say on the day of final inspection? Will there come a time when we'll realize how wrong we've been? Could we have been a more glorious, holy, victorious, and world-changing Church? Could we have fulfilled the great commission sooner? For now, we can only refer to the Church in the Book of Acts as a model and pattern of God's original plan for His Church. Let's take a look at what is commonly referred to as the "primitive Church."

ONE CHURCH

In sharp contrast with the innumerable "flavors" of churches we find in Christendom today, there was only one Church in those days, and those involved in it were "with one accord in one place."

The fragmentation we're seeing in the Church today is, of course, the result of multiple factors. One of the greatest separations in Church history occurred when Martin Luther tried to draw the attention of the so-called "universal church" to the many wrongful practices and traditions it was involved in. The Roman Catholic Church was given a golden opportunity to review what it was doing and make it right. But it chose not to listen, excommunicated Luther, and continued on its path.

Other divisions in the Church can be attributed to human rebellion, selfishness, or an insatiable quest for independence. Any divisions in the Body, no matter who initiates them or however legitimate they seem, are never God's will. In the case of Luther and the Roman Catholic Church, this man should have been hailed as a hero of the Church. Corrections should have been made accordingly, and the Catholic Church would have been the better for it.

AN UNCOMPROMISED MESSAGE

One other aspect worthy of notice is observing how an uneducated, unknown, and unpopular man such as Peter delivered such a powerful message to a mostly hostile audience and got 3000 born again in one day!

Another example of how the primitive Church used the Word as a "two-edged sword" is seen in Stephen, who preached without compromise and cut his listeners to the heart. They had no fear of people who might take it wrong, nor did they entertain the notion of "political correctness."

The preaching of God's Word should never go forth with the intention of making people upset. But the truth needs to be proclaimed in love, even at the risk of hurting someone's feelings.

If a pastor fears the reaction of his congregation to the point of consciously avoiding certain subjects, he is in danger of becoming a hireling. If he refuses to correct unacceptable behavior in his flock and consistently chooses to close his eyes on things God condemns, he may not be suited as a minister who's been mandated by God to perfect the saints.

Thank God for preachers of righteousness in the Church today. They may never draw as large a crowd as some others do. But they'll most certainly hear Jesus call them "good and faithful servants!"

Some churches today are actually promoting themselves as being "seeker friendly." Translation: "Come as you are, live as you please, we will never do or say anything that your flesh might take exception to, we can't help you get closer to Jesus or make you more like Him, but one thing we can promise you-you'll have a good time singing, dancing, and shouting in the social club we call the church."

One of the greatest attributes of the "primitive Church" was its relevancy. It was said about this handful of early believers that they turned the world upside down (Acts 17:1)!

NO MONEY-BUT PLENTY OF POWER

Silver and gold I do not have, but...

Acts 3:6

One clever man said, "When a mosquito bites a Christian, it should fly away singing, 'THERE'S POWER IN THE BLOOD!'"

In the third chapter of the Book of Acts, we find Peter and John going to the temple. Notice that, as was their Master Jesus' custom, early Christians went to church whenever the doors were open. Since God was showing up every time two or more gathered in His name, they couldn't wait to hear what God was going to say and what the Holy Spirit was going to do to confirm His word. There were no fancy personal growth seminars, spectacular Christian concerts, or well-known motivational speakers to attract them to church meetings. They expected God to show up, speak to them, manifest His love toward them, and perform signs and wonders in their midst. Can you believe it? This was good enough for them!

In a day when a majority of churches are cutting back on the frequency of church meetings because of poor attendance, we need to recapture the excitement and expectancy the early Church enjoyed.

Back to Peter and John on their way to the temple . . . there they meet a crippled man who asks them for money, as he'd done to every passerby for so many years. Since they had no money to give this man, the temptation would have been to look the other way. Instead, Peter asks the man to look at them. Aren't you looking forward to the day when any person, whatever their need, can look to the Church for help and actually receive it?

Of course the beggar expects to receive alms from these two. But he's about to receive much more than a few coins. His life is about to change in a most wonderful way! Never again will he have to be a despised beggar. No longer will he have to endure children staring at his infirmity. He will be able to hold a job and even have a wife and family of his own!

At first, the man must have been disappointed when Peter and John told them they didn't have any money to give him. But what a blessing he received when they gave him what they did have. What was that? The healing power of Jesus operating in their lives!

Peter took the yet crippled man by the hand, helped him to his feet, and told him to walk! He didn't pray for him or even lay hands on him! He just told him to get up, in the name of Jesus of Nazareth, and as he helped him stand to his feet, the man walked, ran, leaped, danced, and praised God!

No amount of advertising can possibly replace events like this one! When a man who's been crippled for so many years and has been seen by all who passed this way is miraculously healed in public as spectacularly as this man was, you're sure to grab people's attention.

People literally ran after Peter, John, and the ex-beggar and followed them to Solomon's porch!

NO CHURCH BUILDING, BUT...

One of the most grieving things I've seen in all my life, I witnessed on a recent trip to North Carolina. There they stood, building after dilapidated building, some with enormous holes in the roofs. Some remained standing, helplessly waiting for a bulldozer to put them out of their misery. It seemed as if nothing could stop the vegetation from reclaiming the entire property, which, at one time, were the headquarters of a huge Christian ministry. One monstrous structure that was once a hotel stood like a deathly wounded giant in the middle of a field. Long ago abandoned conference facilities and other grand buildings stood empty. I couldn't help but wonder how much good could have been done around the world with the millions of dollars it cost to build this now defunct "empire?"

Is it wrong for churches or ministries to have buildings? Of course not. Nor is it wrong for the Church to use whatever equipment and tools it needs to get the job done. One of the most joyous things we witnessed in our recent past was the moving of one of the churches we worked with in Rouen to a new facility. The believers had been meeting in the same old building in Rouen, France, for the past 50 years! During the last few meetings there, someone had to actually place several buckets near the platform to contain the water that was dripping abundantly from the ceiling! Was there any question that the 250-plus people of this congregation needed a new building? Absolutely not!

We just need to make sure we don't become real estate developers or stuff collectors.

We'd do well to remember what Jesus told the unfaithful servant who misused what had been entrusted him. (Matt. 25:28)

We already know how Jesus felt about buildings, no matter how grand, when they were not used for their intended purpose. In Matthew 24, the disciples are drawing the Master's attention to the elaborate structure of the temple. Jesus remained totally unimpressed, as He prophesied that the building in question would soon be destroyed.

The Bible tells us that the Church is a spiritual building made up of living stones. Brick and mortar buildings are only there to keep those living stones from freezing in cold weather and for the saints to have an adequate place to meet.

In Europe, many beautiful cathedrals are still standing in large cities today. The only reason people visit them is because of their historical significance or architectural beauty. No one attends church there, nor does anyone usually get saved there. They are just beautiful buildings. At the time they were built, there was actually a heated competition between major cities of Europe for which would have the largest, highest, or most ornate cathedral in Europe. I don't know who won the contest, but I'm sure you'll agree that this was the wrong reason for building these churches.

I thank God for keeping us from purchasing a property we thought we needed for our ministry in France. The facility was to house our full-time Bible school and offices, as well as being used as a major Christian conference and retreat center. It all seemed so right at the time. Besides, the price was more than reasonable. But, praise the Lord, He simply didn't allow it.

When we first started working in the Ivory Coast, more

than ten years ago, it seemed logical for us to purchase or rent a building to house our offices and school there. After all, every international mission and ministry working there had their own building. Again, the Lord wouldn't allow it. The same happened in former Zaire, just before the government of Mobutu was overthrown there. In both instances, we would have lost the buildings and contents because of war and unpredictable political events.

Looking back, I can see how foolish such projects were for us. God spared us from becoming involved in building maintenance and directed us to invest in people rather than structures.

Again, the Church should get all the buildings and equipment it needs and use them for the glory of God. But realize that some churches and ministries have, in fact, created their own "monster" by getting involved in enormous building projects that are consuming all of their time, money, and energy. Anything we endeavor in the kingdom of God that is not of God's creation is the equivalent of a "Frankenstein" that we are solely responsible to feed and keep alive.

How many desperate pleas for money have you heard on Christian television lately? Some are legitimate, I'm sure.

But how many ministers who're in over their heads in expansion projects will someday have to repent publicly like the builder of the defunct property we read about earlier?

As a collective body, the early Church did not own any property. They used whatever facilities they needed for their meetings as God made them available. I truly believe this helped them in "being the Church" rather than going to a church building. Too many Christians today are limiting their church experience to attending church meetings once or twice a week. The Church of Jesus Christ is much too wonderful and far too important in God's sight for us to reduce it to an occasional gathering.

> *Therefore those who were scattered went everywhere preaching the word.*
>
> Acts 8:4

I believe God allowed this persecution of the early Christians in Jerusalem to keep them from getting trapped in the routine of just going to church. He didn't want them to find contentment in fellowshipping with the same people week after week. The Church scattered so that the believers could reach a dying world with the gospel of Jesus.

HUMILITY

Now if you did indeed receive it, why do you boast as if you had not received it?

1 Corinthians 4:7

One noticeable attribute characterizing the early Church was the humility of its leaders.

When the Apostle Peter perceived that the people were crediting him and John for the miracle they had just witnessed, they immediately set the record straight by telling them that it was by the power and in the name of Jesus that the man had been made whole. (Acts 3:12)

Humble leaders in the Church are an "endangered species" today. No matter how popular we become or how many miracles we see in our ministry, we constantly need to remind ourselves that everything we have and everything we get to do, we have received from the Lord.

The Apostle James tells us that God will actually resist the proud (he who takes credit and honor for what God has done). I don't know about you, but it's difficult enough to live and minister in this world without having God resisting you. It's so much better to have God give us the abundant grace He promises the humble. That grace will be sufficient, no matter what we face (James 4:6).

The Body of Christ today needs a good "shot" of humility if we want to carry out the wonderful assignment God has entrusted to us.

BOLDNESS CONCERNING REPENTENCE

Repent therefore and be converted...

Acts 3:19

While we're looking for clues as to why the "primitive" Church had such a great impact on the world of that day, we cannot ignore the direct, uncompromising, "in your face" approach to sin.

We need to remember that in this crowd Peter is addressing are some of the very people who participated in the crucifixion of Jesus. We're not talking about a nice, understanding, warm, and receptive crowd, shouting amen at everything you say!

Peter understood perfectly that "all had sinned and had come short of the glory of God," including himself. Remember Peter's violent denial of Jesus and John's foolish request to be seated next to Jesus in Heaven.

They did not tiptoe around the tulips when it came to sin. As far as they were concerned, there existed no one who didn't need repentance. Whether a lowly slave or a prominent citizen, young or old, rich or poor, educated or illiterate, it just didn't matter. All needed repentance-and fast!

No matter how reluctant preachers become in teaching on the subject and how unpopular a topic it is, repentance is not a "dirty" word, and it is one of the things that will usher in the times of refreshing the Church so desperately needs today (Acts 3:19).

FELLOWSHIP WITH JESUS

And they realized that they had been with Jesus.

Acts 4:13

We just saw that the early disciples were bold in their proclamation of the gospel and exposure of sin. Now let's see what made these uneducated, unpopular former fishermen bold enough to take on an entire crowd. This is even more amazing when you remember that same Peter was afraid of a little girl who thought she'd recognized him as one who'd been with Jesus. Now, this man speaks with such authority and power that more than 3000 people can hear him clearly, and that without the help of a P.A. system!

What made these early disciples so bold that nothing and no one could intimidate them?

The very same people who could tell that Peter and John were by no means qualified to preach to them in the natural sense because they were "uneducated and untrained men" were, however, able to discern that "they had been with Jesus!"

I look forward to the day when unknown, untrained, uneducated, and uncompromising Christians will cause the world to marvel because, undoubtedly, they've been with Jesus (Acts 4:13)!

UNSELFISHNESS TO THE EXTREME

Neither did anyone say that any of the things he possessed was his own, but they had all things in common.

Acts 4:32

At this point in our study of the early Church what is recorded here may appear to some as being a fictional story rather than a historical account. It's true that in our contemporary Church environment, it's very unlikely that something like this could work for very long.

For a period of time, my wife and I actually lived in an environment that was a church's attempt to recreate the atmosphere of the early Church. The experience was such a disaster we still can't believe we allowed ourselves to go through it! Did it fail because we're in the 21st century and God doesn't want this to happen again? Was it because the leader intended to become the guru of a cult? No, but I believe before anything like this should be attempted again, hearts will first have to be radically and miraculously changed by the power of the Holy Spirit!

These people we read about in the Book of Acts really didn't have a life worth living outside of the Church. They now were a living, spiritual cell in a body that had a mission to change the world as they themselves had been changed by the redeeming power of Jesus! They were not their own. As they understood it, the life they now lived was, in fact, the life of Jesus expressed through them. This explains why belongings and earthly possessions meant so little to them. Their identity was so much in Christ that they did not have to rely on riches, social status, or any of the other things our modern society is relying on.

> *Nor was there anyone among them who lacked.*
>
> Acts 4:34

One of the consequences of this remarkable unselfishness was that there was no unanswered need in the Church.

These folks did not have the "us four and no more" mentality. They understood that if one part of the Body was suffering or lacking in any way, the entire Body, in fact, was experiencing pain and need.

There was no need for emotional appeals or graphic descriptions of someone's situation. It was as though the Holy Spirit was causing these people to feel the pain of those in difficulty. They didn't hesitate one moment to do whatever was necessary to remedy the situation.

Why is there so little compassion being manifested toward those in the Church who are geographically or culturally distant today? I believe it's because the Church has lost much of its sensitivity. Also, allegiances to particular denominations seem to be stronger than they are to the Body of Christ. Tragically, many churches are failing to acknowledge their responsibility toward the Body of Christ at large as soon as it's found outside the confines of an organization.

Some churches and organizations have become spiritual "black holes." Whatever human, material, or financial resources come in are exclusively consumed on the church's own projects. Resources come in but are never allowed to come out!

Aren't you glad that it's not up to your heart to decide which part of your body that your blood should or should not flow to?

A pastor friend of mine perfectly described this kind of attitude to me. He was was telling another elderly minister about his intention to take a missions trip to encourage the churches and to hold several crusades on another continent. While he tapped my friend on the head, this old gentlemen told him that if the day ever came when he got every, single person in the U.S, saved, he too might consider getting involved in foreign missions!

You might be surprised at how many pastors are oblivious to the Body of Christ, whenever it's found outside of their own circle of influence or sphere of ministry. How many missionaries have experienced the awkward feeling of suddenly becoming "invisible?" When some pastors discover that the person they've been talking to doesn't belong to their organization and, worse yet, isn't even pastoring a church they could eventually be invited to, the conversation is abruptly interrupted, and the man moves on, looking for a better "prospect."

At least the gentlemen my friend told me about was honest about the way he felt about things outside of his immediate sphere of interest. Politely asking questions or acting as if we we're interested is not the answer. We need Jesus to fill us with His compassion, love, and care for the Church, wherever it's found.

There are actually some churches that operate in total unselfishness today. One example is Pastor Gilles L's church in France. He's taught his congregation that Christians and churches outside of his own local flock are just as much their church family as the people they usually sit next to during the meetings. Whenever a local church in the area needs extra help for a building or some other project, he makes himself and his people available for work! The intercession that goes forth in his church is as intense when it's on behalf of another church as when it concerns the local body. Other churches in the U.S. and other parts of the world also function in a true revelation of the Body of Christ. We praise God for them, and we pray that their unselfish attitude would become contagious and affect the entire Body of Christ.

Every time we partake of the Lord's Supper, we should remember that discerning the Body of Christ also implies caring about the Church outside of our own four walls.

I pray for the day when we will again be conscious of the reality and beauty of the Church at large, when we'll not only feel its pain but also its joys and successes, when we'll be there to help in its time of need and share in its victories, when we'll be just as happy when something good happens at the opposite end of the world as when it happens in our own local church.

NO "EXCUSERS OF THE BRETHREN"

Ananias and Sapphira kept a portion of the proceeds from the sale of their property. They pretended to be giving the full amount of the sale to the Church. Many would consider this to be a fairly mild offense in today's context.

Hold on! Didn't they at least give some of the money to the Church? Weren't they free to do what they wanted with their finances? Who knows, they might even have given the largest portion to the Church! I know of some places where people like these would be given a medal instead of a rebuke!

The way "Pastor" Peter handled the situation reveals the level of holiness and integrity with which the early Church operated.

He knew that this act of deception could affect the entire Church if not handled properly. He was immediately aware of the Holy Spirit's grieving over this infraction.

Notice that Peter did not make an appointment with Ananias and Sapphira to come see him during "office hours?" This involved and potentially affected the entire Church. It was a public affair and thus had to be dealt with publicly.

Thank God, Peter understood the principles of God's power. Had he played down the importance of what this couple did, it is certain that the Holy Spirit would have been grieved by it. It would have been as if "Pastor" Peter had turned the power down in order to spare Ananias and Sapphira. I wonder if the next time the Church needed God's power for a miracle of healing or deliverance it would have been there for them?

I believe that God has made leadership in the Church responsible for the flow of power available to the Church.

We already know through the words of Jesus in John 3:8 that man cannot dictate in which direction the Holy Spirit's power can flow. But leadership can most certainly "regulate" the amount of power it allows the Holy Spirit to exercise in a congregation. One of the most typical and effective ways that leadership can "reduce" the power of the Holy Spirit in a congregation is by preventing the expression of spiritual gifts or by forbidding outward expressions of worship. Of course, it would not be the leadership's intention to diminish the flow of God's power, but it would most certainly be the result!

Observing this unfolding drama, one could think it's a simple case of a leader wanting to make a public example. No, this was an act of the Holy Spirit confirming the wise, uncompromised, and courageous verdict of a godly leader!

When we close our eyes and ignore offenses that potentially affect and hurt the Church, we become what a dear pastor friend of mine calls "an excuser of the brethren." We all know who the "accuser of the brethren" is, and that's the devil. Now, what's an excuser? It's a Christian or church leader who consciously ignores, covers up, or excuses behavior that has already been judged unacceptable by the Holy Spirit! The scriptures call this "partaking in another man's sin."

We may feel that the verdict and sanction on Ananias and Sapphira were way too harsh by today's standards. Had we been there, would we have jumped to the couple's defense? Would we have spoken up, trying to stop Peter from embarrassing these innocent people? Would we have stood in awe at what was happening and with great fear have fearfully made the decision never to lie to the Holy Spirit or to the church? Or, as many Christians are doing today, would we have acted as the "excusers of the brethren?"

Early Christians did not conform to the "pattern of this world," as Paul teaches in Romans 12:2. They didn't limit the demonstration of the power of the Holy Spirit to miracles and healings. They allowed their minds to be renewed and their hearts to be changed by the Holy Spirit. This is why they didn't have their own value system. They scrupulously followed the leading of the Holy Ghost, even when they didn't fully understand where exactly He was taking them.

Allow me to give a perfect example of how the world can influence Christians in a way that is contrary to the Word of God. My wife and I have been working as foreign ministers in France for many years. Anyone who spends more than a few days in that country discovers that the government, the media, and the entire education system are extremely liberal and anti-Christian.

The humanistic environment there has so influenced the way people think that it has developed into a veritable "tradition" or pattern of thought. Even the Church has been affected by it. One of the most classic examples of this influence is in the way French Christians view capital punishment. For almost every Frenchman and nearly all Christians there, capital punishment needs to be abolished in all modern societies. Never mind what God's Word has to say about it (Ex. 21:12-17, Rom. 13:4)!

Now, it is a very natural thing for an ungodly, unregenerated, and emotional human being to think this way. But for a Bible-believing Christian, it's an altogether different story. I can't count the number of discussions I've had with people (and even French pastors) on this very subject. Some even quoted scriptures, attempting to convince me that Jesus did, in some way, do away with this unpleasant but essential duty of a government worth its salt.

The early Church did not insist on doing things its own way. They put aside whatever human-inspired value system they'd been taught, submitting their own opinions and preferences to the lordship of Christ. Jesus is the Head of the Church. When we insist on having our own way in the church, it doesn't matter how strongly we feel about something or how right we think we are-we're creating a "monster" because that's what anything with more than one head really is!

We need to be convinced that God is always right! We may not feel that He is, nor would we handle things exactly the way He does. But then again, we're not God! Another thing we need to settle once and for all is that God does not, nor will He ever, change! God identified Himself to Moses as "I AM." Furthermore, we know that Jesus is the same yesterday, today, and forever. Jesus, the head of the Body, is making no attempt to "adapt" to the ways of the world. He came to save the world and to change it through His Church.

When we attempt to make the Bible fit the ways of modern society, we're effectively diluting the Word of God. What we're doing is, in fact, rendering the Word of God of no effect, in favor of our traditions. This is exactly what Jesus was talking about when He made mention of the salt losing its savor.

As the Church, we desperately need a good dose of seasoning today. We urgently need to regain our relevancy. The world needs to find its moral bearings, and the Church is the only entity mandated by God to do this. How is the world supposed to be convicted about its immorality when a major religious denomination promotes a known homosexual to the position of bishop?

NO "MARKETING" OF GOD'S GIFTS

But Peter said to him, "Your money perish with you, because you thought that the gift of God could be purchased with money! You have neither part nor portion in this matter, for your heart is not right in the sight of God.

Acts 8:20-21

This is the story of Simon the sorcerer's encounter with Peter, the servant of God. This man had believed and had been baptized under the ministry of Phillip. As a new believer, he obviously still had a lot to learn. But what is most remarkable in this story is the way Peter reacted to Simon's offer to purchase the gift of the Holy Spirit with money. This is most significant in light of what's become common practice in today's Church—man's "commercialization" of what God has freely given to the Body of Christ. There are actually seminars available to teach Christian preachers, teachers, singers, and authors how to maximize their income through the marketing and promotion of their God-given talent!

Recently we've even seen the exploitation of certain geographical locations where God had moved in an unusual way. Hundreds of thousands of people traveled there at great expense. Planes and buses were chartered. Volumes of books were sold, and millions of dollars were collected in the offerings. Even if very little of what attracted the masses remains in those places today, some of those who took part in it still travel the globe, trying to "milk" the Body of Christ for whatever they can get out of it.

Simon's motivation for wanting the gift of the Holy Spirit was clearly personal gain. Could it be that the ways of the world have so infiltrated the Church that we can no longer differentiate between businessmen and men of God? The Apostle Peter knew the difference. The strong rebuke with which he addresses Simon the sorcerer should remind us that the Church should never conform to the present world and its greedy ways. Jesus probably won't come back with a whip to chase the merchants out of the temple. He won't have to if we do it ourselves, like He has commissioned us.

By definition, the Church ("ecclesia" in the Greek) means "an assembly called out of and separated from its sur- rounding to perform a particular task or duty." We are mandated by God to "season" our society, just as effec- tively as salt seasons a steak. It's when the opposite happens and it's the steak that seasons the salt that the Church loses its very purpose.

The day is coming (and I pray it will be soon) when the Lord will again use the Church as a standard for right liv- ing for all peoples (Isa. 49:22)!

2

THE LOCAL CHURCH

We know that local churches, regardless of organizational affiliation or geographical location, are a working extension and the visible expression of the Body of Christ.

Before we go on talking about the local church and its purpose and operation, we first need to establish what qualifies as a local church. We already established that whether or not a church meets in or owns a building is irrelevant. So what constitutes a legitimate local church? What are the necessary ingredients that need to be present for a gathering of believers to qualify as a local church?

I would think that the first place to check the legitimacy of what is supposed to be an extension of the Body of Christ is its connection and submission to the head of the Body, namely, the Lord Jesus Christ.

Any gathering of believers whose allegiance and obedience is directed more toward a person or an organization than toward Jesus does not qualify as a church. It may have all the religious appearance, the right architectural design, and a spiritually correct vocabulary but still won't qualify as a local church-at least, not according to God's criteria.

There are several more "essential ingredients" that we'll be looking at in this chapter. Remember that the goal of this study is not to pass judgment on any particular organization but is solely for the purpose of examining ourselves in order to make whatever adjustments need to be made in our own lives and circle of influence. Our goal is to promote greater conformity to the perfect will of God concerning His Church.

A HEAVENLY VISION

Where there is no vision, the people perish.

Proverbs 29:18 (KJV)

Talking about essential ingredients, the first and most important one for a local church is a vision or mission from the Lord. Without it, just as the verse above implies, failure is inevitable. There are way too many casualties in the Body of Christ today. Well-intended, good-hearted people joined what they thought to be a local church, but because of the absence of vision, they found themselves "perishing" a little more each day. The saddest thing about it is that innocent people get hurt in the process. They believed they were getting involved in a real local church. They actually thought they were going somewhere. Great things were going to be accomplished for God. But in the end, they're frustrated and, in many cases, very reluctant or even terribly afraid of getting involved in another church again.

To emphasize the importance of a vision for a local church, allow me to indulge in a culinary illustration. Imagine that you're about to prepare a special omelet. You may want to give it a Mexican, Mediterranean, Middle-eastern, or southern flavor. You will do so by adding different ingredients to your recipe. But no matter what your omelet will become, you will inevitably have to include eggs in your recipe!

Now, when I use the word vision, I'm not talking about a "pipe dream" someone had after eating too much clam chowder! A vision has to be a clear mandate from the Lord concerning the direction a church or ministry is to take. The Apostle Paul refers to this as being a "heavenly vision" when he tells King Agrippa that he's not been disobedient to what Jesus had asked him to do (Acts 26:19). Way too many churches have been started when there really wasn't a clear go-ahead or vision from the Lord at the inception. This is the spiritual equivalent of a conductor inviting passengers to board his train when he himself has no clue as to its destination!

I know of a congregation that was started many years ago by a wonderful man. He had just retired from a prominent position with an international company. He made two very serious mistakes right at the inception of the church. First, because he was receiving a decent retirement from his former company, no financial demand was put on the congregation for the support of the pastor. Second, believing his age would keep him from leading the church for very long, he never communicated any kind of vision to the people or fully stepped into his pastoral role. This wonderful man really thought he was doing the right thing. Today, this congregation is just about as dead as a local church can be. Most people have left, not wanting to sink with what has become a spiritual "Titanic!" What a tragedy. On the other hand, when there's a vision and a pastor who'll assume responsibility for it, nothing can possibly stop such a church from succeeding-not opposition, time, difficulties, or anything else will stand in its way.

> *Though it tarries, wait for it; Because it will surely come, It will not tarry.*
>
> Habakkuk 2:3

In the verse above, the Lord Himself is guaranteeing the successful outcome of a vision, providing, of course, that He is the One who's given it. We need to understand that when church leaders take personal initiatives, the Lord is not bound to help them. Some of these initiatives may be worthy projects, legitimate endeavors, and very wonderful programs. But if they are not God-inspired, they're only good ideas! They may or may not come to pass. However, they should never be introduced as part of God's vision to the people who'll be involved in them. This will only generate confusion and frustration in the local church, as people will be tempted to think that God let them down.

I remember meeting this very nice brother in Christ a number of years ago. In one of our conversations, he told me that he was actually operating in all five ministry gifts of Ephesians 4:11! When he didn't break out in laughter after making the statement, I realized that this man was serious! I don't recall what the outcome of our conversation was, but from that moment on, I knew for certain that I was dealing with someone who had serious delusions about himself and a severe misconception about the ministry of our Lord Jesus Christ.

The next time I saw the brother in question, he reported to me how the Lord was blessing him and was using him. He was pastoring a new church, birthed following a crusade an evangelist friend held in a certain town. I didn't want to "rain on his parade" or judge something before its time, so I refrained from saying anything. However, I couldn't help but wonder how long this was going to last. Within less than three months, the "church" was dissolved, and this "pastor" was already involved in another work. His latest "project" had been started in exactly the same manner, with the same evangelist "rounding up" some sheep for him to pastor. Eventually, three churches were started by these two in less than a year's time. The outcome? You guessed it-the churches closed, the leadership moved on to greener pastures, and the sheep ended up hurt, abandoned, disillusioned and scattered! Please don't judge this brother too harshly because, as I said in the beginning, he was and probably still is a very nice brother. But as the Bible teaches us in Hosea 4:6, this man suffered from a severe case of knowledge deficiency. I pray that he'll be cured from it, in Jesus' name! But I can't help but wonder how many sheep have been hurt in the process and how many will never again join themselves to the beautiful fellowship of believers the local church is meant to be.

TWO PARTS OF THE VISION

Every local church vision will inevitably include two parts: the GENERAL VISION and the SPECIFIC VISION.

The GENERAL VISION is common to all churches, regardless of their size, time of existence, geographical location, or cultural setting.

The very purpose of the Church of Jesus Christ on earth is contained in the general vision. That purpose is three-fold:

1. Reaching the lost for Jesus by whatever means available.
2. The training and development of disciples in the most effective way.
3. Representing and reproducing the Kingdom of God on earth as an "embassy."

Since these are the three essential responsibilities of the local church, it is important that they are given equal attention, being careful not to favor one at the expense of the others.

The first two responsibilities of the Church are included in the last commands of Jesus to His disciples:

> *Go therefore and make disciples of all the nations.*

> Matthew 28:19

and

> *Go into all the world and preach the gospel to every creature.*

> Mark 16:15

The third can be found in Matthew 5:14:

> *You are the light of the world. A city that is set on*
> *a hill cannot be hidden.*

When it comes to the "general" vision, a local church does not have the option of choosing one and not the others.

THE SPECIFIC VISION

This portion of the vision in a given location or social setting is what justifies the very existence of a local church or ministry.

It simply wouldn't make any sense for two churches to function in the same neighborhood, while they share the exact same assignment, that is, beyond the general vision we just talked about. If two churches are doing exactly the same thing in a given location, one of them is completely superfluous. It might be that they belong to different denominations or have different styles of worship, but that still wouldn't justify it. We need to remember that denominationalism is purely man's invention, but God only considers one Church, and that's the one that Jesus Christ is building and of which He is the head. The specific portion of the vision may include outreach to a specific segment of society that other churches are not called or equipped to help. Examples of this would be outreaches to students, prisoners, the homeless, abused women, etc.

Each local church is to perform a particular function as an extension of the Body of Christ. When there's duplication in the functions, frustration and confusion ensue. Aren't you glad you only have one thumb on each hand? Wouldn't it be terrible if you were "all thumbs?"

There needs to be complete freedom for a local church to execute and perform its specific vision. The local pastor to whom God has communicated the specific vision, regardless of how much help and support he may need, must have the freedom to implement his God-given vision. Of course, guidelines and common goals should be agreed upon. But we should be very careful never to hinder the specific expression of the Body of Christ in a particular location or cultural setting. I'm so glad the leadership of the early Church didn't interfere with Paul's methods of evangelization, which called for him to "become all things to all men" (1 Cor. 9:22)!

One of the most tragic things I've witnessed in Africa is the crippling effect of denominational control over local churches. Many local pastors on that continent are forbidden to engage in ministerial relationships outside of the denomination. All buildings and resources are the property of the denomination. Pastors are randomly moved from one location to another, sometimes causing horrendous family situations. No initiative can be taken by the local body unless sanctioned by the foreign board of directors, living thousands of miles away on another continent!

THE TWO PARTS OF THE SPECIFIC VISION

Now that we've established that the heavenly vision has two parts (one general and the other specific), we need to look at certain characteristics of the specific vision.

God instructs Habakkuk to make the vision he's about to receive "plain." Most will agree that plain means simple, uncluttered, not redundant, and to-the-point. God is not, nor will He ever be, the author of confusion. When God communicates His vision for a local church to a pastor, He will only let His servant in on the portion of the vision he is able to handle at the time he receives it.

There is an entire portion of the vision that may not be visible or imaginable, even to the pastor. What the leadership needs to be concerned with is the communication of the portion of the vision God wants to be executed in the foreseeable future. The pastor and leadership also have the responsibility of mobilizing, equipping, and training God's people for the work of the ministry they've been called to within that vision. We will call this the visible portion of the vision.

A good illustration of the dynamics of a local church vision can be found by observing an iceberg. You may only see the portion of the iceberg that rises above the water. But, as the passengers of the Titanic tragically discovered, it's what lies beneath that is much larger and more important.

So it is with the vision. There may be an entire portion that God has not yet revealed. But as the visible portion is obediently executed, the Lord will make more of the invisible known to us. This is why it is so vitally important for a local church to be obedient and faithful, especially during its modest beginnings. It's only when we're faithful in little that the Lord will give us responsibility over more.

There may be times when it would be inappropriate for a pastor to communicate the entire "visible" portion of the specific vision known to him. For example, if it is not plain to him, it will obviously be impossible for him to clearly communicate it to his congregation. Another reason would be that his congregation is not yet prepared to "run" with the vision, once they hear it or read it. As suggested in Habakkuk 2:2, not only do God's people have to have the ability to comprehend what is presented to them, but they also need to be ready to "run with it." There may be some preparation and training necessary in order to bring the people around so that they will know what to do with the vision, once they hear it.

A local pastor should not be surprised or discouraged if his congregation doesn't receive the vision enthusiastically and unanimously as he had hoped. "Visitors," for example, cannot be asked to "run" with the "specific vision," but they can certainly participate in the "general vision," as long as they're attending the local church. Christians who're still seeking God about their permanent assignment to a local body cannot be expected to participate in the specific vision with the same level of zeal and enthusiasm. However, those who're directly concerned, such as the elders, deacons, and those involved in the ministry of helps, should at the very least receive it and be ready to execute it.

> *...according to the effective working by which every part does its share.*
>
> Ephesians 4:16

This brings us to the next point concerning the vision. To what extent should individual Christians be involved in a local church vision?

The verse quoted above talks about every part doing its share. When God reveals His vision to a local assembly, it's a signal that He has already made provision for its realization. This would not only include the spiritual gifts, material resources, and finances but also the human skills necessary to carry it out.

This is what the scriptures refer to as "diversities of gifts" in the Body. This is where discernment in leadership is so important. One the responsibilities of the pastor is to identify the diverse gifts present in his congregation. He then needs to match those gifts with the portion of the vision that needs it most, and finally, he needs to provide training that will enable these gifts to be used most effectively.

Beyond the qualifications for elders and deacons we find in 1 Timothy 3:1-7, it is imperative that those working in these capacities be in full agreement with the vision they're supposed to uphold. In fact, their very ministry within a local church should be contingent upon their understanding of and agreement with the vision the pastor has received from God. It would be inconceivable for elders and deacons to continue as such, once their disagreement has been made known. In Amos 3:3, the Bible asks the question, "Can two walk together, unless they are agreed?" The answer? They can't, or at least, they shouldn't!

So how do you deal with an elder who's no longer in agreement with the vision? Of course, it's never easy to tell someone they'll no longer be able to serve in a public capacity in the church. One of the ways leadership can prevent painful misunderstandings and avoid hurtful separation later is with clear communication early on. A prospective elder or deacon must be aware that the ministry position he's about to embrace is directly tied to his wholehearted involvement and support of the vision of his local church. Should there come a time when agreement is no longer present, the elder and the pastor should be able to mutually agree to a change. When this is done in a spiritual and mature way, there will be little or no disruption to the church.

What should a pastor do when a person with a particular gift can no longer fulfill his assignment? This is especially difficult when someone has been occupying a particular position for many years. They have become somewhat of a "permanent fixture" in the church, and it seems like things just wouldn't be the same without them. Meet sister Olga. When this old saint started out as the secretary of the church some 30 years ago, she was God's answer to the pastor's prayer. But today, with the growth of the church, a constantly increasing workload, and rapidly changing technology, poor sister Olga, who's still typing with only two fingers, just can't keep up anymore! There are several options open to the pastor, but only one of them is the right one. He could, of course, keep things just as they are by allowing sister Olga to continue in her position. Of course, the work won't get done correctly, but at least sister Olga will be happy and so will her many friends and family members in the church. Another option would be for him to assign helpers to sister Olga. They would do all the actual work, but sister Olga would retain her position and get credit for the job done.

This reminds me of a funny situation in a small North American community. The local emergency service of this small town has been manned by the same two volunteers for many years. Today these men are well into their seventies and are refusing to retire. Whenever they're called upon to lift a person unto the emergency vehicle, the town has to recruit other volunteers to help these two get the job done. It will probably be a sad day when these two gentlemen are finally retired, but honestly, when volunteers have to be called in to do what the volunteers are unable to do, it's time to replace the volunteers!

The Apostle Paul was confronted with a similar situation involving Barnabas and his cousin (Acts 15:37-39). Because John Mark had abandoned them in Pamphylia sometime earlier, Paul decided not to bring him along on their next journey. This was not about settling a score or about teaching this young minister a lesson in commitment. His decision was solely based on obedience to the heavenly vision. There could not be any compromise or emotional consideration when it came to God's vision. Paul knew perfectly well that by making this decision, he was risking his friendship with Barnabas. But he also knew that compromise in this situation meant disobedience to the vision of God. When the Holy Spirit later prompted him to invite Mark to join him, he might have had an emotional struggle with the idea, but regardless of how he felt personally, he was going to obey the heavenly vision, no matter what!

A REAL PASTOR

The second ingredient in our recipe for a legitimate local church is a pastor. He may be a more powerful evangelist than he is a teacher. He may be a strong administrator, or he may excel at surrounding himself with people who have administrative skills. He may be more comfortable teaching small groups than he might be addressing an entire congregation. But he will most definitely have the ability to gather and lead God's people.

Elders, such as those Paul commanded Titus to appoint in every city, had to meet certain criteria before being considered for that position. While a pastor needs to meet the same qualifications, what distinguishes him from other elders is the responsibility for the execution of the vision toward God. In a sense, Moses was the legitimate "pastor" of the people of Israel, while he lead them out of Egypt and through the wilderness. While a number of elders helped him to carry out this enormous task, "Pastor" Moses had to ultimately be God's spokesman to His people and in the end was directly responsible for carrying out the Lord's vision for His flock.

Even when God's people did things without Moses' knowledge, it was Moses' responsibility to inform them, instruct them, and correct them.

Being a pastor is probably one of the hardest things God will ever ask anyone to do. The awesome responsibilities and the daily pressures can be overwhelming at times. But if that's what the Lord has called someone to do, there are only two options open to them-do it, or disobey!

If someone has any uncertainties or doubts about a pastoral call, they should not "volunteer" for that position. It's hard enough when there's a deep conviction about the calling of God and when His grace is present to perform it.

Often in today's Church it seems that the pastor is the only minister who's entitled to a salary. But that should not be a sufficient reason for an evangelist, prophet, teacher, or apostle to engage in a ministry he's not been called to. This is the equivalent of spiritual prostitution and is one of the many sins we, as the Church, need to repent of today.

I praise God for the "repositioning" of ministries that is taking place all over the world in the Body of Christ today! From Europe to Asia, from North America to Australia, and from South America to Africa, men and women of God are obeying the Holy Spirit by allowing Him to place them in their proper ministry. In many cases, this repositioning is in total disregard of financial considerations and often means less enviable positions and considerably less comfortable living conditions.

It would seem obvious that no one should engage in a ministry they've not been called to. You might be surprised at how many Bible college or seminary students actually enroll in those schools for the sole purpose of someday becoming pastors! One of the first things we teach our Bible college students is that we will do everything in our power to equip them for the ministry to which they've been called. But we're quick to inform them that we cannot train them for a ministry God hasn't already called them to. We can train people for the ministry and give them a diploma to sanction their achievements, but we can only confirm or validate what God Himself has ordained.

No amount of training or collection of diplomas or taped "prophetic" utterances will make anyone into something God has not already called them to!

AN AMBASSY OF GOD'S KINGDOM ON EARTH

*You are the light of the world. A city that is set on
a hill cannot be hidden.*

Matthew 5:14

One of God's main purposes for the local church is to be a visible expression, not only of the Body of Christ but of the Kingdom of God as well.

Whenever unsaved people come into contact with the local church, either by meeting a group of Christians or an individual belonging to a local body, they should in some way be exposed to the realities of the Kingdom of God.

The American Embassy in Paris is located in the heart of the city near the Champs Elysees. As long as you remain outside of the compound, you most definitely know you're in France. But anyone entering the building immediately experiences the feeling that he's entered another country. The architecture, furnishings, government employees-everything there reminds you of the United States, right down to the bathroom fixtures! It's a little like visiting the U.S. without ever leaving Paris.

This is the way it should be when unbelievers come to our local churches. For example, this is where they should discover what real love is. Their understanding of it is completely distorted. When they witness the loving interaction between Christians and become the recipients of God's love through the Church, they may experience (maybe for the first time in their lives) what genuine love is! The same goes for peace. Most people in the world have come to accept peace as the state someone is in when there is an absence of conflict. But Jesus made a clear distinction between the sort of peace the world can experience and the kind that's "beyond understanding" that only He can provide! As world-battered people come into our places of worship, may they discover and enjoy what we've received from our Prince of Peace.

It's amazing the number of people, from all over the world, who apply for permanent residency in the U.S. every year. Far more are being turned down than there are people being issued visas. Even with the tightening of border security following 9/11, thousands of illegal immigrants are still flooding into the country every year. Why would they leave their familiar surroundings? Why do they risk their lives crossing dangerous borders? Why do they come to a land where the customs are different, where the language is foreign to them, and where there's no guarantee of a job? Simply because they're convinced that life will unquestionably be better for them, once they get there.

Why do you think thousands joined the Church in the early days? Very simple-people heard not only a teaching about the Kingdom of God but actually witnessed practical Kingdom living among God's people. They saw it in their devotion toward God and His word, in their love for each other, and in their fervency in prayer.

One of my pastor friends, now leading a great church in Australia, described it best. He shared with me that the greatest responsibility of leadership is to implement a Kingdom "culture" in the local church. He had just returned from the Ukraine, where he had done just that. I understand that his church today is one of the strongest bodies of believers in the entire nation!

> *Now when the queen of Sheba heard of the fame of Solomon, she came to Jerusalem to test Solomon with hard questions.*
>
> 2 Chronicles 9:1

Even though it is found in the Old Testament, the story of the Queen of Sheba is a wonderful example of how a local church should function. Imagine for a moment that Solomon is the pastor of a local church. This queen is not there to make a social call. She apparently has some hard questions, and she fully expects this pastor to give her the answers she needs. She didn't come empty-handed, but she's not giving any of her camels, gold, spices, or precious stones away-at least not right away.

"Pastor" Salomon must have made a very good impression on this lady-so much so that she's opening her heart to him and telling him "all she had on her mind!" Imagine this! None of the questions took Solomon by surprise. He didn't have to make an appointment with her in six weeks so he could think about his answers! No, he answered her there and then! And to think that he had not even been baptized in the Holy Spirit!

In verse three, we're told that the Queen of Sheba "saw" the wisdom of Solomon. We all know that wisdom is not a visible object that you can touch or see. So what did this queen see to make her say that? I'm so glad you asked! We're told in verses three and four what she really saw. It is related to us that the food on the tables, the seating of the officials, the attending servants, and the cupbearers in their robes simply overwhelmed her! That's how she saw Solomon's wisdom.

She apparently had received some "advertising" for Solomon's "church." But she was certain that what was said about it was just another exaggeration. After seeing this ministry with her own eyes, she now exclaims in paraphrase,

"What I read about this ministry doesn't even begin to tell the story! What I've seen here far surpasses what I've been told!"

It is then, and only then, that she gives the order for the gold, precious stones, and other gifts to be given to King Solomon's ministry!

I can't wait for the day when people from the world will be so overwhelmed by what they see that they'll give glory to the Lord and bring their most precious gifts to the local church that operates in the wisdom and power of God's Kingdom!

> *...to the intent that now the manifold wisdom of God might be made known by the church to the principalities and powers in the heavenly places.*

Ephesians 3:10

Again, as the verse above clearly defines, this is one of the three main purposes for the Church. It is not an "either/or" situation. We have been mandated by God Himself to represent Him and to live our lives according to the "culture" of His Kingdom.

> *The wealth of the Gentiles shall come to you. The multitude of camels shall cover your land, The dromedaries of Midian and Ephah; All those from Sheba shall come; They shall bring gold and incense, And they shall proclaim the praises of the Lord.*

Isaiah 60:5-6

The day is coming when this prophecy will be fulfilled in the Church. But it will only happen in the midst of local assemblies that are functioning as "embassies" of God's Kingdom on earth. The challenge is great, but we can do it, in Jesus' name! The Lord has never asked the Church to do anything He's not given us sufficient power and grace to accomplish.

Before closing this chapter, I need to say one last thing. An embassy serves a purpose when it is operating outside of its own country. The Church can only fulfill its mandate if it operates outside the confines of its religious structure. We're to be the salt of the earth. It's high time the Church came out of her "salt shaker!"

3

MINISTRIES IN THE CHURCH

And He Himself gave some to be apostles, some prophets, some evangelists, and some pastors and teachers...

Ephesians 4:11

To insure that His bride would be spiritually ready and adequately prepared when He returns, Jesus specifically gave the five ministry gifts to the Church.

All saints of God need to be regularly exposed to these five ministries if they are to be perfected, equipped, and edified.

Jesus went through a lot of trouble to make these five ministries available to us. Of course, a local church pastor will spend the most time ministering to his flock. But he certainly shouldn't be the only ministry his people are ever exposed to.

This can be a problem for a small church. The pastor may feel that the church cannot afford to have these ministries come in. Believe me, the church cannot afford not to have them come in. Furthermore, if an apostle, prophet, evangelist, or teacher makes such financial demands that it would keep him from blessing a local church, as a pastor, I don't think you should expose your people to them in the first place.

You probably noticed that the apostle appears first on every biblical list of the five ministry gifts. People often interpret this to mean that the ministry of the apostle is the most important, followed by the prophet, the evangelist, and so on. But this is an erroneous and carnal way to look at these ministries. Some men of God today go as far as inscribing these titles on their calling cards, expecting some sort of veneration or special honor from God's people.

The passage of scripture below shows that the ministries of the apostle and of the prophet are foundational to the building of the Church. But as everyone knows, once the foundation is laid and the building is up, the foundation is generally covered up and no longer visible.

> *...having been built on the foundation of the apostles and prophets...*
>
> Ephesians 2:20

HOW IT'S SUPPOSED TO WORK

We already determined that the reason the apostle is named first is not because he's better or more important than the other ministries. Just as in 1 Corinthians 12:29, the reason is that he's the first ministry sent by God to begin a new work. The five ministries are named in a chronological order of intervention and not in a hierarchical order of importance.

To illustrate this point, allow me to use the illustration of the erection of a new building. Before you hire a builder, purchase the construction material, or buy the furniture for your new house, you'll absolutely need to know where it's going to be built! When it comes to the planting of a local church, this is where the apostle comes in. He is the one sent by God to determine and confirm whether a new church should be established in a particular location. He is the one who is called upon to lay the spiritual cornerstone of the church, determining its spiritual "blueprint," height, and breadth. I understand that many churches have started without the help of such a ministry. But unless the founding pastor was himself flowing in an apostolic authority, chances are these churches are running at a very low spiritual "speed" or may no longer be in existence.

THE PROPHET

The prophet is the second ministry a local church absolutely needs, especially in the beginning stages. He is the equivalent of an architect in the building environment. God uses this ministry to give the initial direction of the vision to the local church. Again, the local church pastor may be one who flows in the authority and the anointing of a prophet. Nevertheless, these two ministries are essential to the establishment of a new church, since they are the foundational ministries upon which the spiritual building will rest.

We spoke of the necessity of "real pastors" leading local assemblies. The same goes for true prophets giving direction to the Church. We're given many examples of false prophets throughout the Bible. Unfortunately, they are not extinct, by any means. In the Old Testament, when people discovered that a prophecy didn't come to pass, they were to throw the prophet down a steep cliff, thus putting an end to his career!

We're under a new covenant now, and we shouldn't push false prophets off tall buildings! But I don't think the Church should keep on listening to someone who's wrong as often as he's right.

If we are prepared to receive true prophets; if we're ready to hear what they have to say on the Lord's behalf;

if we refuse to listen to those who only prophesy what we want to hear, God will surely send us prophets who'll clearly give us His directions.

THE EVANGELIST

Now, where does the evangelist fit in? I'm so glad you asked! Just like during a normal construction project, once you've determined where you're going to build and what you're going to build, you'll need to think about getting some material together so you can start building. This is the evangelist's job. He's anointed by God to provide the "living stones" the church needs for its construction. Of course, every saint in the church needs to do the work of an evangelist and bring in new souls. But the evangelist is anointed to bring them in, in a much greater number.

THE PASTOR

We now come to the next ministry on our list, the pastor. God has given him a most wonderful and awesome responsibility-that of "trimming," "cutting," "polishing," and finally "fitting" those "living stones" exactly where God wants him to place them.

Of course, his job would be easy and wonderful if all the living stones were as easy to shape as clay in the potter's hand. But this is often not the case. These stones we're talking about are living stones. These stones have feelings, emotions, opinions, and sometimes many unresolved issues that the pastor has to deal with. This is why the pastor needs to be particularly developed in the areas of patience and understanding.

One of his most important responsibilities is that of a shepherd to the flock. Of course, Jesus is the Chief Shepherd of the Church, and the local pastor needs to fully submit to Him. But the pastor is asked to lead and feed his flock, following the example of Jesus we're given in the twenty-third Psalm. He will lead the flock into "green pastures." This means that he will always deliver fresh spiritual food to his sheep-not stale, reheated, or lifeless messages but "hidden manna" from Heaven!

He will also gently and carefully lead God's people to "still waters." This means that he will avoid highly controversial subjects. He will stay clear of any political propaganda or commentary of newspaper headlines. He will simply stick to preaching God's word.

A pastor is also mandated by God to be the "doorkeeper" of the local church. You'll notice that Jesus is addressing "the angel" of each of the seven churches in Revelation 2:1 through 3:22. These "angels" are, in fact, the pastors of these seven churches. Not only is the pastor the channel by which God speaks to His people, he's also responsible for what is being taught God's people from his pulpit. If something potentially harmful or biblically wrong is preached in his church, not only is it the pastor's right, it's his duty to bring whatever correction is necessary. No more than a mother would allow a stranger to feed her children poisonous food should a pastor allow someone to "contaminate" his flock. On a broader scale, an apostle is also a "doorkeeper" to an entire nation. The Lord will hold him accountable for the teachings he allowed the pastors in his care to be exposed to. The Lord reminds me of a great apostle of a European nation. This man's influence and popularity didn't cease to grow in the last 20 years of his ministry! During the last two or three years of his life, however, he made some grave mistakes. He imposed several controversial preachers and even some "shady" characters to the large group of pastors he was overseeing. When I questioned him about his reasons for doing this, his answer was, "Pastors should be mature enough to retain what's good from these ministries and reject what's not." His answer was absolutely correct. But he forgot that as an apostle, he still had the responsibility of a "doorkeeper" for his nation. Sadly, he went to be with the Lord less than a year after we had our conversation.

THE TEACHER

This is the last of the fivefold ministries on our list. Now that the living stones the evangelist has brought in have been trimmed, cut, polished, and fitted by the pastor, what could be the next and final step? The stones will have to be set in conformity with a spiritual "plumb line." This is where the teacher comes in. His job consists of verifying that everything was built in conformity with the "master plan," the Bible.

This is where the maturity of the pastor and his godly respect for a ministry gift other than his own is so very important. It may have taken him years to finally build a "wall" that by some miracle won't blow over with the first wind of opposition! It takes a fairly secure pastor to let another minister come in and "inspect" what he's worked so hard to build. There is even a chance that some of the "walls" will have to come down and then lovingly rebuilt on the solid foundation of God's Word.

He who receives a prophet in the name of a prophet shall receive a prophet's reward.

Matthew 10:41

It is extremely important that all five ministries Jesus gave to the Church be received as gifts by local church leadership. There are tremendous rewards attached to this. But, as you'll see in the following verses, we stand to suffer severe consequences if we fail in this area.

> *"O Jerusalem, Jerusalem, the one who kills the prophets and stones those who are sent to her! How often I wanted to gather your children together, as a hen gathers her brood under her wings, but you were not willing! See! Your house is left to you desolate; and assuredly, I say to you, you shall not see Me until the time comes when you say, "Blessed is He who comes in the name of the LORD!"'*

Luke 13:34-35

I don't know about you, but I sure don't want my house to be desolate. I also want to see Jesus return with power and glory and a host of angels when He comes back for His bride.

This is why I say, "Blessed is the apostle, the prophet, the evangelist, the pastor, and the teacher who comes in the name of the Lord!

4

A TEAM OF WORKERS AND DISCIPLES

Then He said to them, "The harvest truly is great, but the laborers are few;

Luke 10:1-2

Now that we have a heavenly vision, a pastor who'll be responsible before God to lead the church in its realization, and other fivefold ministers who'll come alongside to help, we need people to carry it out.

It's interesting to notice that Jesus did not entrust His ministry (the Church) to the people who were merely following Him. Some were closer to Him than others. Some had been healed by Him, and others had relatives raised from the dead by Him. But that's not whom He choose to carry out His purpose on earth. No, He chose twelve who'd witnessed His resurrection, but most importantly, twelve who'd followed Him as disciples.

While everyone should be welcomed and feel loved and accepted in the local church, in the end, it will only be the true disciples who will have the determination, zeal, and perseverance to bring the vision to pass.

> *You therefore must endure hardship as a good soldier of Jesus Christ. No one engaged in warfare entangles himself with the affairs of this life, that he may please him who enlisted him as a soldier.*
>
> 2 Timothy 2:3-4

In many ways, disciples are like soldiers of an army. They have given up their personal ambitions in exchange for a higher common goal. They are prepared to suffer hardship, if it means furthering the cause. They have forfeited the comfort of familiar surroundings and are ready to subject themselves to unknown and sometimes even dangerous conditions.

Again, a local church should not ignore or neglect those who're not yet qualified as disciples. The same goes for those who may not yet understand what it means to be a disciple. Jesus Himself didn't give the multitudes "a cold shoulder" but rather had compassion on them. Notice, however, that He handled things very differently, depending on whether He was addressing the crowds who followed Him for what they could get or the disciples who'd followed Him because they believed there was no life worth living outside of Him. The dedication of the disciples is so vividly expressed through Peter when he tells Jesus in John 6:68, "Lord, to whom shall we go? You have the words of eternal life."

We're told in Mark 4:34 that Jesus didn't speak to the multitudes, except in parables. On the other hand, He took extra care in explaining the parables to His disciples.

There's a great lesson here for us to learn as the Church. We need to care for and love everyone who comes in. But we cannot assume that everyone in our church is automatically a true disciple. One of the greatest effects the Holy Spirit had on the early Church was the change that occurred in the hearts of these men. They went from being believers to becoming true disciples. It's interesting to note that Judas was known as one of the "disciples" of Jesus. But when it was all said and done, we realize that he obviously didn't have the heart of a disciple. It becomes evident that his motivation for following Jesus was so he could have free access to the bag holding the ministry's money! We will study the qualifications of a true disciple in the following paragraph. But the most important of all is the change of heart and attitude that needs to take place in the life of a believer.

Just because someone is capable of handling a responsibility, doesn't mean he or she should be given a position in the church. We cause great damage to the Body
of Christ when we ignore the principles of discipleship.
The example of Judas should be a reminder to us. Jesus
knew perfectly well that Judas did not have the heart of
a disciple when He "recruited" him as one of the twelve. I
am convinced that this is the very reason He only
entrusted him with the least important assignment in
his ministry, holding the money bag. You'll remember
that Jesus didn't rely on what was in that bag, even
when it came time to pay His and Peter's taxes!

Although everyone in the flock should be treated with
love and respect, we should never give important assign-
ments to anyone who doesn't have the heart of a disciple.

QUALIFICATIONS OF A DISCIPLE

I have no doubt that every born-again Christian truly
desires to be a disciple. If you're reading this book, I'm
sure that this is your heart also.

The first thing we need to know is that becoming a
believer and joining a church does not automatically
make a disciple out of us.

For us to better understand what a disciple is, we need
to look again at the qualifications of a soldier.

No one engaged in warfare entangles himself with the affairs of this life, that he may please him who enlisted him as a soldier.

2 Timothy 2:4

One of the first things the armed forces require of a soldier is for him to rearrange his priorities. I'll never forget when I received my orders to serve in the French paratroops many years ago. To say the least, the convocation did not come at an opportune time! I had just married my wife Josette in the month of December. Shortly afterwards, we found out that my little wife was pregnant! The orders said I was to join my unit in early January! For some reason, we believed it was useless trying to explain to the military administration that this just wasn't a good time for us. Even at this young age, I had enough sense to realize that I was in military service now and that I had to reorganize my entire life as a soldier. In a way, not having a choice in accepting or refusing the assignment made it easier. One of the major differences between being drafted in the military and volunteering as a disciple is the in the latter case, tragically, you can say no!

As I mentioned before, there is a great variety of people attending a typical local church. Some may be new converts, still needing the "milk" of the Word, on their way to becoming spiritual adults. Others are totally satisfied in simply attending church or being "consumers" of God's blessings. Others, who used to serve as fervent disciples, have surrendered their spiritual "uniforms" because they feel too old, too discouraged, or too hurt to serve in the church.

While I was serving in the military, there was a multitude of things I could think of that were more challenging, more rewarding, and certainly more fun to do than what my lieutenant or sergeants asked me to do. But I just couldn't bring myself to point them out to them. Somehow I had a feeling they just wouldn't understand my questioning their intelligence and might just put me in the brig!

One of the ways you can find out if you're a disciple or not is to ask yourself the following question, "When asked to choose between an activity I have planned and something church leadership asks me to do, what's my response?"

If you're a disciple, the answer is simple, "I'll rearrange what I had planned, get the job done, and then think about how and when I'll do what I had originally planned."

A regular churchgoer will find all kinds of reasons or excuses for not doing what they've been asked to do.

When a churchgoer hears that something needs to be done in the church, he will only consider it in the light of his own agenda. If leadership can motivate him sufficiently and if there happens to be an open slot on his calendar, he may actually consider the matter. What is considered a suggestion to a churchgoer is considered an order to a disciple!

But, you see, a disciple of Jesus Christ realizes that he doesn't really have a life of his own. He has willingly and gladly offered not only his soul and heart but also his body as a living sacrifice to the Lord (Rom. 12:1). He understands that the only life worth living is the life and ministry of Jesus flowing through him. Along with the sacrifices a disciple makes, there are plenty of rewards as well. One of the greatest of them all is the one Jesus promised those who'd rearrange their agenda and give priority to serving the Kingdom of God. All the things which had to be put on the proverbial "back burner" for the gospel's sake are handled by the Lord Himself! Disciples discover very quickly that God handles these matters much mote quickly and more efficiently than they could have ever done themselves! What a tragedy when Christians become so consumed by their own agenda that their God-given assignment is left unattended and unfulfilled!

And do not be conformed to this world, but be transformed by the renewing of your mind, that you may prove what is that good and acceptable and perfect will of God.

Romans 12:2

When reading the previous verses in Romans 12, it becomes obvious that for such an attitude change to happen in the life of a believer, there needs to be a complete transformation in his thought pattern and perception of his surroundings.

As long as someone sees the things of the Church with the eyes of the world, he will resent the fact that someone would even dare ask him to alter his personal plans.

But to a disciple, it's the most "natural" thing to do. He recognizes that this is the "good, acceptable and perfect will of the father" for his life (Rom 12:2).

One of the greatest difficulties a local pastor faces in leading a body of believers is when the people of his church have not yet made the transition from being attending believers to participating disciples.

It's easy asking a disciple to do something, with the assurance that he'll do it with excellence, as unto the Lord. But it's a totally different matter when dealing with an attending believer. This Christian's personal agenda needs to be taken into consideration. There's also a risk he might get offended when asked to do something. This is why many pastors often choose to handle the job themselves. There may be qualified people in the church who could do it and do it better. The pastor just refuses to take the risk of offending someone and can't bear to see them leave.

There's no reason to panic when this happens in the early years of a local church. It is a very normal pattern in the growing process of a young congregation. It turns into a tragedy, however, when after many years, the church still doesn't have true disciples to count on.

There was an occasion when many people stopped following Jesus because He'd said something that deeply offended them. It didn't really surprise the Master, since He was dealing with the multitudes. But then He addresses His disciples and asks them if they too would abandon Him. I'm convinced that Jesus never thought for a moment that these men would leave him. Why? Because they were disciples!

> *Whatever your hand finds to do, do it with your might.*
>
> Ecclesiastes 9:10

ATTITUDE OF A TRUE DISCIPLE

One of the distinctive attitudes of a disciple is that he'll do whatever needs to be done. He looks to the Lord rather than to men for recognition or rewards. He's therefore ready to take on any assignment that comes his way.

This is so evident in the attitude of Stephen. He's just as fulfilled and blessed as a "waiter" as he is to be a preacher and an evangelist.

If we insist on picking and choosing what we will and will not do in the church, could it be that we have not yet developed the attitude of a true disciple?

What is also obvious in the attitude of the early disciples is that they were not looking for titles. True, the apostles laid hands on them publicly after choosing them. But nowhere does it say that a title was given them, nor did they really care!

But let your 'Yes' be 'Yes,' and your 'No,' 'No.'
Matthew 5:37

Another characteristic of a true disciple is that he finishes what he has committed to do.

Too many Christians volunteer to do things in the church, without considering the time, effort, and sacrifice it will take to get the job done.

Not only will a disciple complete the job, he will do it in an excellent and timely manner.

> *So his armorbearer said to him, "Do all that is in your heart. Go then; here I am with you, according to your heart."*
>
> 1 Samuel 14:7

These are the most inspiring words a disciple can ever say to his leader! As you meditate on this scripture, make a decision to become a true disciple. Let the Holy Spirit renew your mind concerning Christian service. Refuse the world's perception that if you serve, you are being used by men. Go on to discover that there's nothing more rewarding and fulfilling than to serve God in your local church!

5

POWER AND ANOINTING IN THE CHURCH

As we already discovered, one of the distinctive traits of the early Church was its power. People may not have understood their message or agreed with their lifestyle, but one thing is sure-they couldn't deny the miraculous power working in them.

> *And seeing the man who had been healed standing with them, they could say nothing against it.*

> Acts 4:14

The question that concerns us is why was the power of God demonstrated in such an extraordinary and sustained manner in the early Church?

Some will argue that these were special times and that God had a particular purpose for making such tremendous power available to the early Christians.

I refuse to believe such a notion. How could our God, who says we shouldn't do anything by our own power, ask us to do anything without His Spirit in these end times?

'Not by might nor by power, but by My Spirit,'

Zechariah 4:6

No, God's hand is not too short nor has His power been diminished toward the Church. The problem, I believe, lies elsewhere.

I don't know if you know how an electrical transformer works. The only reason I even remember is because I worked in a factory that built them when I was much younger. The purpose of a transformer is to reduce high voltage electricity to a lower, more manageable power. This is done by placing many "obstacles" in the way of the current so that it alters its flow. The power eventually comes out reduced on the other side of the transformer.

I believe this is exactly what happened to the power of the Holy Spirit in the Church! One compromise at a time, one leader's scandal swept under the rug after another, the Church has become the spiritual "transformer" of God's power on the earth!
If we are to restore the power of the Church to the level God intended it to be, we absolutely need to reverse the

current trend. This means that we first need to repent of all the compromises and occasions when we actually became accessories to other Christian's sins. It is an absolute necessity that we assume our responsibilities in this matter.

> *Assuredly, I say to you, whatever you bind on earth will be bound in heaven, and whatever you loose on earth will be loosed in heaven.*

Matthew 18:18

6

UNITY OF THE BELIEVERS

Now the multitude of those who believed were of one heart and one soul.

Acts 4:32

As previously mentioned, there was but one Church in those days. One might think that achieving unity would be a cinch in this kind of environment. I wouldn't be so sure. The devil probably knows scripture better than you and I. He understands that one isolated Christian can "only" put a thousand of his demons to flight. But he's aware that two can disperse ten thousand of his troops! Do you think for a moment that Satan would hesitate to throw a "monkey wrench" in the harmonious cooperation enjoyed by the early Church? He knows only too well that when an entire assembly, as in the Book of Chronicles, or when two or three simply gather in the name of the Lord, Jesus Himself shows up in the midst of them. I'm convinced that the devil did everything in his power to prevent the continuity of unity in the primitive Church.

Just as today, there must have been plenty of opportunities for early Christians to disagree about one thing or another. The difference? They just didn't allow these things to come between them and divide them. They did what every mature Christian couple should do-they may not agree on everything, but they won't allow anything to come between them and separate them from each other.

What was happening here is that these Christians were so taken in by this new "abundant life" they had recently discovered, they just refused to waste time or energy on doing anything else. Their focus was so much on sharing what they found in Jesus, they simply wouldn't be distracted with criticism, quarreling, or divisive discussions.

> *And the glory which You gave Me I have given them, that they may be one just as We are one: I in them, and You in Me; that they may be made perfect in one, and that the world may know that You have sent Me.*

John 17:22-23

We discovered earlier that the power of the Holy Spirit came upon the Church to enable early Christians to become effective witnesses throughout the world. Here,

Jesus tells us that the glory of the Father is given the Church so we can become one in Him and one in the Father.

Again, just as I said concerning "having everything in common," this kind of unity will never happen unless a drastic spiritual transformation takes place in the Church. Of course, many attempts have been made to achieve unity in the Church throughout history. But most of them have failed miserably.

Ecumenism is only one of the many failures we could talk about, but we won't.

One of the main causes of failure in unity initiatives is when the basic motivation for wanting to unite is wrong. Some people and organizations are only interested in gathering people to themselves in order to achieve some intended project. This is not at all what Jesus was talking about in the verses we just read.

Another reason for failure is that unity, the kind Jesus is talking about, is something we have to work on consistently and effectively. It's just not going to happen by itself.

If there's one thing the devil will work the hardest to prevent, it is unity! He almost succeeded in getting the people of Babel to build a tower that would reach to Heaven. He didn't forget that it was unity among these people that made this possible. God Himself had to intervene and confuse their language to put an end to it.

> *How could one chase a thousand,*
> *And two put ten thousand to flight,*
>
> Deuteronomy 32:30

THE POWER OF UNITY

When Christians get together in unity in the name of Jesus, something powerful takes place. The Lord Jesus actually shows up! Remember the hundred and twenty in the Upper Room? If two or more get in agreement concerning a specific request, they set in motion the most powerful dynamics available to mankind (Matt. 18:19-20)!

Notice I didn't just say, "when Christians get together." They actually need to get together in unity. Paul severely rebukes the Corinthian church for getting together for the worse and not for the better. Why would he say that? There were divisions among them (1 Cor. 11:17-18).

WHERE DOES UNITY START?

It would be so easy to just sit there feeling sorry for not seeing more unity and the Church wishing that some-body would please do something about it.

Unity is the responsibility of every child of God. Before we can see an outward manifestation of unity throughout the Body of Christ, it will first have to be a reality at home. This is where unity begins. We're only fooling ourselves, thinking that we can tolerate a divided home and still expect a united local church. As goes the family, so goes the local church.

True unity ought to be the trademark of the local church. People without Christ have no concept of what unity really is. They should find it among Christians who work, study, and grow together in the local church. The only kind of "unity" most people are familiar with is the political process by which people are recruited under the banner of a person or organization to help them achieve certain objectives.

LOVE—THE GLUE THAT MAKES US ONE

The unity between the Father and the Son is purely based on love. Our motives for uniting within the local church should be the same.

As you read the instructions on a glue container, you'll notice that before applying the glue, you must make sure the two surfaces you're about to bond are perfectly clean. The same goes for godly unity. There cannot be any unspoken resentment or unresolved issues between those who intend to unite. Love is the glue, but truth is what allows a perfect bond! True friends should have the liberty to tell each other the truth in love if they ever want to grow in unity.

A local church that understands godly unity and has mastered it to some extent can then pursue unity with other parts of the Body in the region. This will extend beyond periodical gatherings of pastors praying together and shouldn't be limited to occasional multi-church meetings when a well-known speaker comes to town. Pastors will actually become friends. They will be there for each other in times of need. When something good happens to a church they're united with, they will celebrate as if it had happened to them.

One of the favorite tools of the devil for preventing unity in a city is past offenses. It may be that someone in the past has committed a mistake. But because things were never corrected or forgiveness was never granted, relationships seem irremediably severed.

These things can go on for years and years. Sometimes the people originally involved have gone to be with the Lord years ago. But the unsettled offense still stands in the way of any kind of unity between the churches who inherited this mess! Unless one pastor decides to go to the other and both work diligently at reestablishing the dialogue, unity in the city will never be achieved.

*that they may be made perfect in one, and that
the world may know that You have sent Me,*

John 17:23

How will the world ever know that Jesus was truly sent
by the Father to save mankind if we cannot be one with
those who're part of the same Body in our city?

PURE MOTIVES—PRIORITY #1

This brings up an interesting question-were the scribes
and Pharisees of Jesus' time believers or unbelievers? If
they were believers, why didn't Jesus work with them?
The answer? Jesus knew their hearts and recognized
that their motivations were wrong. They only wanted
Jesus with them to control Him and to promote themselves.

People unite for the wrong reasons in the political arena
all the time. Candidates who were fierce enemies yesterday join forces to defeat another whom they perceive as
a greater enemy yet!

WITH WHOM CAN WE BE UNITED?

Another hindrance to achieving true unity is the failure
to understand to whom we're to be united. The Bible
teaches us not to be unequally yoked together with

unbelievers (2 Cor. 6:14). This, of course, has to do with those who're outside of the Christian faith. This does not mean that we shouldn't have anything to do with non-Christians. It simply means that we cannot be involved with them at the same level as if they were believers. We must keep in mind that unity of the Spirit (Eph. 4:3) is only possible with those with whom we already enjoy unity in the faith (Eph. 4:13).

MAJORING ON THE ESSENTIALS

Can two walk together, unless they are agreed?

Amos 3:3

This verse talks to us about agreement. But what are the things we need to agree on? Obviously, this has nothing to do with personal preferences or individual opinions.

For us to walk in unity, we'll need to agree on the things that are important to God.

As we have already learned, the devil will do everything he can to keep us from walking in unity. One of the most effective ways he has devised is to draw our attention to minor differences and use them to separate us. Thank God we're not identical clones. Praise the Lord for the differences that make us unique. Aren't you glad that just because men and women are different, it doesn't keep them from becoming one? In fact, procreation would be impossible, were they identical.

UNITY OF THE SPIRIT

Having unity of faith simply means that we're not to be united with unbelievers. Unity of the Spirit is somewhat more complicated. This will require much more discernment and sensitivity to the Holy Spirit.

> *This girl followed Paul and us, and cried out, saying, "These men are the servants of the Most High God, who proclaim to us the way of salvation. And this she did for many days. But Paul, greatly annoyed, turned and said to the spirit, "I command you in the name of Jesus Christ to come out of her." And he came out that very hour.*
>
> Acts 16:17-18

You must admit that Paul had to have a good dose of spiritual discernment to deal with this servant girl like he did. Did she not follow them for several days? Didn't she say all the right things? Not only did he not ask her to join them, he actually cast a demon out of her!

Just because someone is using the right "vocabulary" and is saying what you want to hear doesn't mean we should walk in unity with them. I'm not talking about being suspicious of everybody but just being careful to what "spirit" we are uniting ourselves.

> *But He turned and rebuked them, and said, "You do not know what manner of spirit you are of."*
>
> Luke 9:55

Jesus Himself had to rebuke His disciples when they yielded themselves to a spirit other than the Holy Spirit! There was no hesitation here. This situation demanded immediate attention. Jesus dealt with it, and everyone could walk in unity again!

The early apostles understood this principle perfectly. They realized that if they were to walk in spiritual unity and enjoy the power that comes with it, they would have to deal severely with any spirit that was not from God.

> *Every kingdom divided against itself is brought to desolation, and every city or house divided against itself will not stand.*
>
> Matthew 12:25

We do not have a choice in the matter. Unity is not an option. Remaining divided, as we are today, can no longer be tolerated. If we are to stand as the glorious Church Jesus is coming back for, we will have to unite with those the Lord wants us to walk and work with.

Imagine a human body, dislocated, with organs and members scattered all over the place. What a terrible sight! But this is what the Body of Christ looks like today. We must pray that the Lord Himself will breathe on us again and that the Body will stand on its feet, as an exceedingly great army (Ezek. 37:10).

CONCLUSION

If you finished reading this book and still have unanswered questions, I believe that the main objective of this book has been reached-getting you, the reader, to ponder on the subject of the Church. It took us many years to reach our current condition. We probably won't become a "winning Church" overnight. I'm well aware that it will take more than our good intentions, a few weeks' time, and a book such as this one to reverse the terrible effects of aging and to get rid of the "spots" and "wrinkles" we have collectively accumulated over the past 2000 years. But may God supernaturally redeem the time that we may quickly become the glorious Church He has intended us to be from the beginning.

What's important is to start somewhere. It could be that you've been satisfied simply being a church member all these years, but now you've been challenged to become a true disciple. Maybe you've made a decision to become an "ambassador" of Christ to the world. You're determined to demonstrate Kingdom realities in your daily life to motivate others to meet the King of Kings. Perhaps you've made the decision to reach out to others in unity. From now on, you will extend a hand of fellowship to brothers and sisters outside of your local church and denominational boundaries.

Whatever it is, do something for Jesus that you've never considered doing before. If you do, let me encourage you by saying that you truly have ears to hear what the Spirit is speaking to the Church today! I also pray that the Holy Spirit will give you a revelation of the Church as God Himself sees it. May He give you such love for the Body of Christ that you'll begin to clearly see why Jesus so willingly gave His life for His beloved Bride.

Let us not stay in an attitude of denial, as the Laodiceans did. As we hear God's voice, let us not harden our hearts to His pleas, as we're admonished in the Book of Hebrews. Make the decision right now to do whatever you can, at your level, to help the Church get ready for Jesus' return. When the last trumpet sounds, you will be so very glad that you did!

> *Let us be glad and rejoice and give Him glory, for the marriage of the Lamb has come, and His wife has made herself ready.*
>
> Revelation 19:7